America's National Capital

America's National Capital

A guide in pictures and text to Washington, D.C.

by E. John Long

4 maps by Rafael Palacios

Doubleday & Company, Inc., Garden City, N.Y.

Photograph on Title Pages by Hubert A. Lowman

Table of Contents

OUR NATIONAL CAPITAL
Focus of the Free World

Romans, at the height of their imperial power, proclaimed: "All roads lead to Rome!"

Today Americans may say the same thing of Washington, D.C., with perhaps more justification. For this magnificent city on the Potomac has become the focus and nerve center of the entire free world.

Yet, incredibly, it seems to the stranger that Washington presents no outward show of power or strength. It has no breath-catching skyscrapers, nor heavy industries, nor bustling commerce, nor even any great displays of private wealth. With its beautiful downtown parks, dignified monuments, shaded boulevards, and neoclassical architecture, Washington appears to be more a sedate showplace than a world capital that can call the turn in the near and far places of the globe.

History has no counterpart for this urban beauty who flexes her muscles when necessary, very much in private, and whose power, wealth, and influence all are derived from without. Nor does the record reveal any instance of a large community coming ahead so far so fast. Washington actually is a mere stripling, a youngster so to speak, among the national capitals of the world, and even among some of the cities of the United States.

What is the story behind Washington's meteoric growth from a mudbank village-capital of thirteen struggling former British colonies to its present stature as the metropolitan hub and shining hope of all those who believe in democratic ideals? And all within a little more than a century and a half!

There probably could be many answers, but one thing is certain. Washington, in its rapid development into a center of world power, is not a copy of any other national capital. From the beginning it was a planned, made-to-order seat of government, set up within its own small federal district, although the metropolitan city has long since bulged out of the District of Columbia.

Most Americans are unaware that, from the close of the Revolutionary War, when the congress was in Philadelphia, until 1800, the youthful United States had five "capitals" or meeting places of the Congress—Princeton, Annapolis, Trenton, New York, and Philadelphia once more. For various reasons, none of these cities offered an ideal seat of government for the new nation. Southern states protested that they were all too far north. Certain state laws hampered the Congress, as did local ordinances. Business interests and unpaid veterans in these centers harassed the Congress with their special demands. After the Constitution was adopted, the establishment of a new city was considered.

The location was resolved, finally, at a dinner party. After much discussion and sound Madeira wine, Hamilton, of New York, agreed to a southerly site if Jefferson, of Virginia, would consent to Congress assuming the Revolutionary War debt of the colonies.

President Washington, noting that the junction of the Potomac and the Anacostia Rivers stood almost halfway between New England and Georgia, pinpointed the exact location, and Congress passed a bill for a federal city and capital on July 17, 1790. While the capital is named *for* George Washington, it was not named *by* him. The first President called it simply "the Federal City," and the name "Washington" did not come into general use until after his death. Even today "Washington" is merely a mailing and timetable address; local government is conducted in the name of the District of Columbia.

In the beginning the new federal District of Columbia straddled the Potomac, and included two small but thriving communities—the town and port of Alexandria, Virginia, and Georgetown, at the head of tidewater, on the Maryland side. The rest of it was largely rolling farm land, woods, and swamps.

When Congress and the rest of the small government's agencies arrived from Philadelphia in 1800 to set up housekeeping, the new capital must have looked very unpromising indeed. Only a fragment of the Capitol was completed, and but a part of the White House. Other government departments were scattered about, and few houses had been built. Sale of lots dragged, even after government workers began to arrive. Tradesmen and speculators alike seemed to consider the whole venture as visionary and a bad risk. Congressmen and diplomats lived in Georgetown, and commuted by omnibus through muddy or dusty streets to Capitol Hill and government offices.

These must have been trying days

indeed for all who still felt that the idea of a separate federal district was sound and necessary. Most foreign visitors scoffed openly, and ambassadors considered themselves punished if they were assigned to Washington (today it is the most sought-after diplomatic appointment).

Up until the time of the Civil War, Washington grew quite slowly. It really was just another sleepy southern town, enlivened only when the Congress was in session, and not much even then. But, after the panting and defeated Union troops had staggered back into town from the First Battle of Bull Run or Manassas, Washington suddenly awakened and met its destiny. Overnight the capital became an armed camp, ringed with forts and earthworks. Its streets teemed with troops, lobbyists, camp followers, and hundreds of opportunists seeking government jobs, contracts, or favors. As the command, supply, and communications center of the North, Washington had finally become the *real* capital of the United States, although it had to lose eleven of them in the process. Its population jumped from 61,000 to 250,000.

Again, during World Wars I and II, Washington experienced further growing pains. Temporary wooden office buildings and living quarters sprang up like mushrooms along the Mall and in other downtown park areas. The New Deal of the 1930s, with its vast increase in federal agencies, brought many economists, technicians, and other specialists, as well as hordes of clerical workers, to the District.

Meanwhile scientific, patriotic, and union-labor organizations began to find the city hospitable, as did those planning conventions and conferences, large and small. New nations spawned by the World Wars added their embassies and legations to the diplomatic scene, giving Washington's official and social life a truly international flavor, previously missing. Trade missions and enlargement of the press corps brought in still others. Always a good tourist town, Washington, with the advent of parkways and superhighways in nearby states, has become the mecca of the traveling vacationer.

Today, Washington ranks ninth in population among cities in the United States with Government its largest "industry."

One cannot but wonder what the founding fathers, and especially the early capital's many detractors, would say if they could see today's dynamic city at the head of the Potomac's tidewater. Much that Washington's pioneer planners hoped and strove for has come true, indicating that they planned well. Much remains to be done, particularly in clearing away some of the nation's worst slums. But a start has been made on this, too, proving that Washington today still has its enlightened dreamers and planners, whose sights are set as high as were those of Washington, Pierre Charles L'Enfant, and all those visionaries who founded this capital city in which every American can take pride.

THE CAPITOL
AND THE
CONGRESS

Washington, the capital, now spreads over so much territory and has so many exciting facets that the stranger, particularly the tourist whose time and funds may be limited, hardly knows where to begin.

Most native Washingtonians agree, however, that there is no better place to start than that majestic edifice on a hilltop, the fountainhead of the laws which rule the nation, the Capitol. Its great iron dome commands every vista, day and night, and, if Congress is in session, you can see and hear history being made—in the debates over laws that affect the lives of all of us.

Except for the White House, the Capitol is the oldest government building in the District of Columbia. Its cornerstone was laid by George Washington himself, on September 18, 1793, seven years before the Congress and the infant federal government moved from Philadelphia to the shores of the Potomac. Like Rome, the Capitol was not built in a day, but many years. It is hard to believe that two little boxlike buildings, connected by a passageway, served as Capitol until John Quincy Adams' administration, when a low-domed central hall was completed.

The Capitol's first photograph,

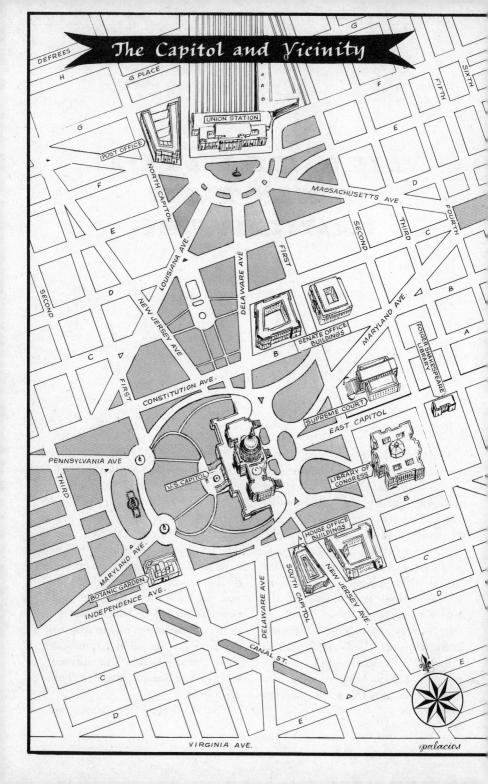

taken shortly before the Civil War, shows the present big dome emerging, and the House and Senate wings extending on each side. Few changes have been made in the historic building since then. Work is now under way, however, to move the central façade and east portico forward. When this was first proposed, it aroused a storm of controversy, the hottest architectural squabble since President Truman added a balcony to the White House in 1947.

The Capitol has been called, justifiably, "the wonder building of the world." To Americans every nook and cranny is steeped in tradition and history. If your visiting time is limited, or if the great structure overwhelms you, take the official guided tour. At 25 cents, it is the biggest quarter's worth in all of Washington.

Your guide will point out some of the nation's best (and worst) sculptures in Statuary Hall, where each state is represented by a statue of one of its famous sons. Several of the massive paintings in the rotunda and over the marble staircases look familiar. They should. Depicting great moments in the history of America, they have been widely reproduced in textbooks and magazines. If, finally, you need refreshment, drop down to the House Restaurant and order a steaming bowl of its celebrated bean soup.

Since Puerto Rican fanatics used the House for a shooting gallery in 1954, a pass from a member of Congress is needed before you can enter the visitors galleries of the House or the Senate. It is not difficult to get. Members of Congress have their offices in large buildings flanking Capitol Plaza. You can ride (free) to the Senate Office buildings on Washington's only subway, or walk through an underground passageway to the House offices.

Go to the office of the Representative from your district, or the Senator from your state, identify yourself, and a pass will promptly be issued. You probably won't see the Congressman, who may be attending a legislative committee meeting at a morning hour or may be in his seat in Congress in the afternoon. Congress usually convenes at the stroke of noon. Don't be alarmed at the occasional loud ringing of bells. These are roll calls, summoning members to a floor vote from meetings, offices, the restaurants, or wherever they may be.

Were it not within the shadow of the Capitol, the stately French Renaissance edifice of the Library of Congress might attract more attention. There is no question, however, about the fame of its internal treasures, for this is not only the largest library in the United States but also one of the greatest reservoirs of organized knowledge ever assembled.

While its main function is to assist the Congress, the Library also registers copyright claims of writers, musicians, producers of motion pictures, and others. It prints catalogue cards for other libraries. Such services bring in the tidy sum of over $2,500,000 annually, proving that government is not all "outgo."

The Capitol

The one building that dominates the beautiful city of Washington is the Capitol, which stands on Capitol Hill, highest point in the city. Home of both the Senate and the House of Representatives, the structure itself, which contains some 430 rooms, is 751 feet long, 350 feet wide, with its dome rising to 285 feet. Topping the dome is the 19-foot bronze statue of Freedom, a symbol of hope to free men everywhere. The 36 columns which surround the lower part of the dome represent the states in the Union at the time this impressive structure was designed.

The Congress

The Senate, which is in the north wing of the Capitol, and the House of Representatives in the south wing, make up the Congress, the legislative branch of government. John C. Calhoun, Henry Clay, Daniel Webster, William E. Borah were all articulate members of this august body. Because of its more generous proportions, the House—pictured on the page opposite and top left—is used for joint sessions of Congress. President Eisenhower is shown here at his State of the Union Message in January 1955. The mace, a staff of 13 ebony rods bound together by a silver band and topped by a silver globe and eagle, is the House's most treasured possession and symbol of government authority. It is at the right of the Speaker's desk. A recent and unique addition to the Capitol is the non-denominational prayer room, lower left, which is used by members of Congress for prayer and meditation.

Statuary Hall and the Rotunda

Statues of distinguished citizens from nearly all the states are in Statuary Hall. Unusual acoustics of the Hall make it possible for a whisper on the far side of the room to be heard in the center. The Rotunda, below, directly beneath the dome of the Capitol, is 95 feet in diameter. It is decorated by the mural frescoes of Constantino Brumidi, and the historical paintings of the Revolutionary period by John Trumbull. Gutzon Borglum's famous head of Lincoln is also here.

The Great Day

Inauguration Day is the 20th of January, and almost all inaugurations in the more than a century and a half that Washington has been the seat of government have taken place on the steps of the main entrance on the east front of the Capitol. At the far right is a general view of the inaugural scene of January 20, 1949, when President Harry S. Truman was sworn into office. After taking the oath of office, the President delivers his inaugural address and then almost immediately afterward leads the colorful parade from the Capitol to the White House. This public procession is perhaps one of the most exciting parades anywhere, and thousands line historic Pennsylvania Avenue to get a glimpse of the President. Here President Eisenhower waves a warm greeting to the crowds that pack the sidewalks as he leads the Inaugural Parade of 1953.

Capitol Dome is seen from a charming flower-banked terrace.
View from Dome itself, below, is impressive.

House Office Buildings are on both sides of
New Jersey Avenue.

Tourists as well as Senators take the subway that connects
the Capitol with Senate Office Building, above.

Above figures in fresco of Capitol Dome were completed in 1953 by
Allyn Cox. Replica of Capitol is beneath the Rotunda.

Fine collections of orchids, azaleas, citrus fruits are
found in the Botanic Garden.

Owned and operated by the Government, the Botanic Garden
is open weekdays and Saturday morning.

Rococco main building of the Library of Congress, left, contains
unusual marble stairways elaborately decorated.

Library of Congress, which also includes the newer Annex, above,
holds some 11,400,000 volumes plus manuscripts, maps, prints.

Floodlit Capitol Dome is spectacular on any night—even a rainy one.

At night the Capitol Plaza's fountain is a rainbow of color.

A mantle of snow enhances the beauty of the Capitol.

Washington's crack network of communications includes gentlemen of the press, radio, television, buzzing switchboards, and the Capitol pages.

THE SUPREME COURT

Until 1935, the United States Supreme Court met in the old Senate Chamber of the Capitol. This was not a happy situation. Under our Constitution, the judiciary, represented by the Supreme and other federal courts, is an independent branch of the government, one of three; the others are the legislative or Congress, and the executive, headed by the President.

Since 1935 our chief tribunal has had a magnificent home of its own, flanking the Library of Congress and facing the Capitol across the tree-shaded Plaza. Although fully functional, it is built in the classical style, with lavish sculpturings that depict the development and preservation of our legal rights. Incidentally, the massive white edifice is said to contain more marble than any other single building in the world.

Like the Capitol, the Supreme Court Building has been the scene of many fateful hearings and decisions—actions that have drastically affected the lives of all of us. To see the nine justices of the United States Supreme Court in their august black robes file into the Supreme Court chamber and seat themselves in a line at the mahogany bench against a deep red velvet curtain is one of the most stirring spectacles in Washington. Because the number of public seats is limited to 144, the line forms early on the days when momentous decisions are expected.

The first Monday in October is the traditional opening day for a new Court session, which lasts until June. The Court sittings begin at noon, and public seats are on a first-come, first-seated basis. As the justices take their seats, the crier impressively chants:

Oyez, Oyez, Oyez! All persons having business before the Honorable, the Supreme Court of the United States, are admonished to draw near and give their attention, for the Court is now sitting. God save the United States and this Honorable Court.

The building itself is open whether or not the Court is in session.

For each of the Justices there is a suite of three rooms—private office with bath, secretary's office, and filing room. A basement garage and private elevators enable the Justices to enter and leave the building with the privacy befitting their dignity and office.

In keeping also with the high station of the tribunal, lawyers appearing before the Court at one time had to be attired in formal day dress. If one came unprepared, there was an emergency wardrobe closet, containing a medium-sized tail coat, stiff collars of assorted sizes, and ties, in the clerk's office. Today, lawyers appearing before the Supreme Court are expected to wear a black or navy blue suit and a vest.

New Justices appointed by the President are sworn in with the oldest (1808) Bible still in use by the Federal Government. Quill pens, recalling Colonial times, must be used by the Justices when they sign the decisions of the Court. The quills are ten inches long, pure white, and two of them are placed on a pad before each Justice. A former cavalry officer in New Haven, Conn., supplies the Court, obtaining the quills from the feathers of Emden geese. And, while the Justices are quite strict in their interpretation of the law, they may look the other way if a visiting lawyer wishes to take one home as a souvenir!

The nine carved figures on the pediment of the Supreme Court Building symbolize the Justices who make up the Court. Justices are appointed by the President with the advice and consent of the Senate.

Justices of the United States Supreme Court are seated, left to right: William O. Douglas, Hugo L. Black, Chief Justice Earl Warren, Felix Frankfurter and Tom C. Clark. Standing: Charles Evans Whittaker, John Marshall Harlan, William J. Brennan, Jr., and Potter Stewart.

Regarded by many to be the handsomest building in Washington, the Supreme Court, above, reflects the dignity and grandeur of its office.

The Supreme Court Chamber measures 82 by 91 feet and is 44 feet from floor to ceiling. The Justices' Bench is set in front of a deep red curtain.

Chief Justice Vinson administered the oath of office to President Eisenhower for his first term; President Truman is at the left.

Charles Vernon Bush became the first Negro U. S. Supreme Court page.

Chief Justice Warren swears in Mr. Eisenhower for his second term.

MR. PRESIDENT
AND THE
WHITE HOUSE

It is a moot question in Washington whether the Capitol or the White House holds first interest. As the residence of the President, perhaps the White House has the edge. Every President *except* Washington has slept there. Ex-President and Mrs. Washington did make an inspection tour of the unfinished mansion, however, shortly before General Washington's death in 1799.

Three Presidents were temporarily "dispossessed" during their terms of office: Madison, when the British burned the building in 1814; Theodore Roosevelt, during the renovation of 1902; and Truman, during the virtual reconstruction of its interior, from 1948 to 1952.

The cornerstone of the Executive Mansion, as it was originally known, dates from October 13, 1792, 300 years after the landing of Columbus. Although there are older houses in Georgetown, the President's home is the earliest of all government buildings in the District of Columbia, and the first to be completed in the form we find the main structure today.

Compared to the huge, glittering palaces used by European and Asian rulers at the time it was built, the White House is a simple, almost unpretentious dwelling place. Then, as

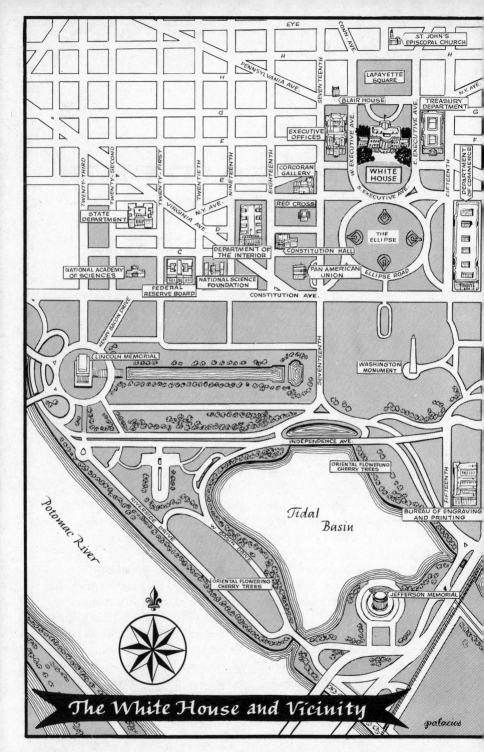

The White House and Vicinity

now, it stands as a symbol of democracy, although the extensions of Presidential duties and responsibilities in recent years have forced the Executive Office of the President to seek additional operating quarters in the former State, War and Navy building next door.

When its first Presidential occupant, John Adams, arrived in 1800, only six rooms were ready for use. Mrs. Adams wrote disconsolately to a friend: "There is not a single apartment finished. We have not the least fence, yard, or other convenience, without, and the great unfinished audience [East] room I make a drying room of, to hang up clothes. The principal stairs are not up, and will not be this winter."

During the tenure of James Madison, the Executive Mansion took on an air of elegance and became the center of great activity with Dolly Madison the brilliant leader of the city's social life. Through her efforts a good deal of the Mansion was richly furnished but this was not to last. The British troops which arrived in Washington in 1814, were indirectly responsible for the name "White House." Following the burning of the edifice, the marks of the fire on the sandstone walls were concealed by painting the whole building white. But it remained the

"Executive Mansion" until the administration of Theodore Roosevelt, when "White House" appeared on the President's stationery and the term became official. Oddly enough, dignitaries and other invited guests arrive or depart from the "back door," 1600 Pennsylvania Avenue. The White House was planned to face the Potomac, but it has no accessible doors on this front or on the southern side.

The general public may visit parts of the White House and its grounds, without charge or pass, even while the Presidential family is there. Of course, the President's quarters are securely shut off, but you may stroll through the East Room, State Dining Room, the Red, Green and Blue Rooms, and basement corridor. The House is open Tuesday to Saturday, between 10 A.M. and noon. Picture taking is permitted in the grounds, but not within the Mansion.

Not far from the White House rise three of the noblest structures ever erected to the memory of man—the Washington Monument, the Lincoln Memorial, and the Jefferson Memorial. Beautifully planned and executed, these tributes to three great Americans draw millions of visitors each year. The pages following indicate a measure of their beauty and grace.

Press Conferences

The President's news conference reached its full flowering during the administration of Franklin D. Roosevelt and has been ably continued by his successors, President Truman and President Eisenhower. These conferences are held in the executive wing of the White House, and are attended by reporters representing newspapers throughout the country, foreign newspapers, press associations, radio, and television. Other top officials in government frequently call press conferences—Vice-President Nixon is pictured at left—making Washington perhaps the best-covered city in the world.

The White House (north view) at 1600 Pennsylvania Avenue, N.W., is
the official residence of the President of the United States.

President Roosevelt is shown addressing a group assembled on the south lawn.

South portico of the White House contains the controversial Truman balcony.

The Family Dining Room, above, is found on the first floor. China used
by past Presidents is displayed in the China Room, below.

The Green Room, left, is used for informal receptions. Note the
Great Seal woven into the carpet.

Many American publishers present books to the White House Library.

Diplomatic Reception Room is a charming oval-shaped room.
The Red Room, right, is handsomely decorated with red silk damask.

White House's State Dining Room can seat more than 100 guests.

Gold and white East Room, largest in the White House, is 79 feet long.

The Main Lobby, looking toward the East Room, contains
presidential portraits and state seals.

This sylvan glimpse of the White House is from the
steps of the Treasury Building.

A considerable staff is needed to process the three to four
thousand letters that arrive daily at the White House.

The President's private living quarters are on the second and third floors. Room above was President Truman's second-floor study.

Incoming White House mail and packages are carefully screened. Executive Office Building, right, is opposite the President's Office.

Distinguished Visitors

Winston Churchill, Queen Elizabeth and Prince Philip, General Charles de Gaulle, Queen Juliana of the Netherlands, Anastas Mikoyan of Russia are just a few of the distinguished foreign visitors who have come to Washington in recent years. Washingtonians are quite used to the stream of colorful personages that continually flows through the city. Eastern potentates and their entourages as well as distinguished Americans, such as General Douglas MacArthur, are not unfamiliar sights on the city's broad avenues. Foreign guests frequently reside at Blair House on Pennsylvania Avenue during their stay in Washington. King ibn-Saud of Saudi Arabia, King Peter of Yugoslavia, former Prime Minister Mackenzie King of Canada, to name only a few, have all stayed there.

The Lincoln Memorial

One of the most awe-inspiring and breath-taking memorials of grace and beauty to be found anywhere in the world is the Lincoln Memorial in Washington. Dedicated to the Great Emancipator, the Memorial is designed like a Greek temple, with 36 Doric columns representing the states in the Union at the time of Lincoln's death. On the south wall is inscribed the Gettysburg Address, and on the north wall, the Second Inaugural Address. But the dominant feature of the building is the magnificent, realistic figure of Lincoln seated in the center of the open temple. Nineteen feet tall and executed by sculptor Daniel Chester French, it embodies the qualities that are forever associated with the great man— compassion, warmth, strength of character, and an ineffable sadness. At night the figure is superbly illuminated: then is considered by many the best time to view it. Designed by architect Henry Bacon, the Memorial is visited by as many as 1,600,000 people each year. It is open every day except Christmas and Labor Day.

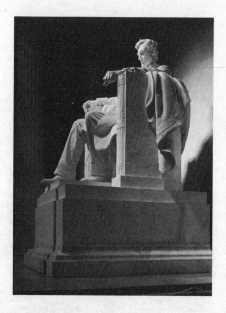

Viewed from any position, or at any time of year,
the Lincoln Memorial presents a picture of grandeur and beauty.
The Reflecting Pool, 2,000 feet long and 160 feet wide, and
bordered by rows of beautiful English elms, mirrors the Memorial.

A Famous Landmark

The tallest stone structure in the
world, the Washington Monument
soars 555 feet, five and one-eighth
inches into the sky. The pyramid at
the top contains the inscription,
"Laus Deo" or "Praise be to God."
The walls, 15 feet thick at the base
of the Monument, taper to
18 inches just below the pyramid.
Memorial stones inside the shaft
were sent from many countries
of the world as well as
our own states. Stones
carved with tributes to George
Washington were contributed by
Turkey, Greece, China, Japan, Swit-
zerland, and Brazil. The cornerstone
for the Monument was laid in 1848
but public controversy, and then
the Civil War, delayed its
completion for many years. The
difference in the color of the
marble where work was stopped and
then resumed after 24 years is
apparent to the visitor. The
Washington Monument was finally
opened to the public in 1888. More
than 1,000,000 visitors each year
visit this magnificent obelisk
dedicated to the father of our
country.

The beautiful cherry trees along the Tidal Basin bloom in the spring. The graceful Washington Monument rises in the background.

Fourth of July is celebrated in spectacular fashion near the Monument.

These lovely trees were a gift from the City of Tokyo to Washington in 1912.

Hardy souls have been known to climb the 898 steps to the top of the Washington Monument but most visitors prefer to ride up in the elevator and walk down. Walking down is particularly rewarding because it is possible to see the memorial stones with their inscriptions clearly from the staircase. A really breath-taking view is obtained at the 500-foot level and this spectacular glimpse of the city is never forgotten.

The Capitol with its striking dome, above, and the White House and its 18 acres, below, are seen here from the top of the Washington Monument.

The Thomas Jefferson Memorial, below, in its beautiful setting on the Tidal Basin, can be seen from the south window of the Monument.

The Jefferson Memorial

Designed after the Pantheon in
Rome, which Jefferson
admired so much, this tribute to our
third President contains
a striking 19-foot figure of
him sculptured by Rudulph Evans,
and panels that quote
from Jefferson's most famous
writings including
the Declaration of Independence.

Set on the south shore of the Tidal Basin, the Jefferson Memorial
was dedicated on the 200th anniversary of Jefferson's birth.

The classic beauty of the Memorial is striking in any season.

THE FABULOUS SMITHSONIAN

There is just one word for the Smithsonian Institution: "fabulous." Not only is it the largest educational and scientific organization of its kind in the entire world, but, with 5,000,-000 visitors annually, one of the greatest of all meccas for tourists, young and old. Its multitudinous activities range from the operation of several of the nation's foremost museums and art galleries, the Washington Zoo, and distant scientific observatories, to publication of hundreds of scientific papers, laboratory research, and the sending of expeditions to the far places of the earth.

The Smithsonian Institution, a private foundation established with the bequest of $550,000 from the will of James Smithson, is under government guardianship, and is charged with operating ten government bureaus in addition to other duties. The original Smithson endowment has been raised to $3,500,000, although about $1,700,000 of this is restricted to projects chosen by the donors.

The U. S. National Museum, National Collection of Fine Arts, National Zoological Park, Bureau of American Ethnology, National Air Museum, Astrophysical Observatory, International Exchange Service, Canal Zone Biological Area, Freer Gallery of Art are all administered by the Smithsonian Institution. The National Gallery of Art is also included in the Smithsonian group but is administered by a separate board of trustees. In addition to these, the Weather Bureau, the Bureau of Fisheries, and the Geological Survey are Smithsonian children, but are now located elsewhere.

Few of the Smithsonian's hundreds of thousands of annual visitors realize that it is not only a great showplace

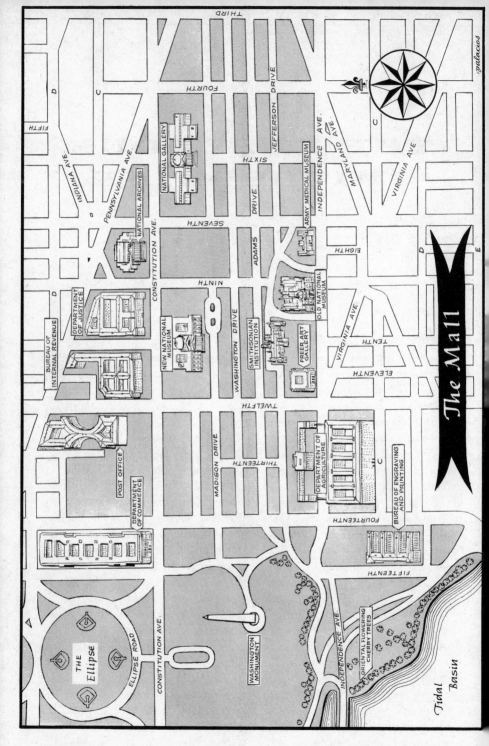

The Mall

THIRD

FOURTH

NATIONAL GALLERY

SIXTH

JEFFERSON DRIVE

D

C

INDEPENDENCE AVE.

MARYLAND AVE.

VIRGINIA AVE.

C

D

E

FIFTH

INDIANA AVE.

PENNSYLVANIA AVE.

NATIONAL ARCHIVES

CONSTITUTION AVE.

SEVENTH

ADAMS DRIVE

ARMY MEDICAL MUSEUM

EIGHTH

DEPARTMENT OF JUSTICE

NINTH

WASHINGTON DRIVE

SMITHSONIAN INSTITUTION

OLD NATIONAL MUSEUM

FREER ART GALLERY

VIRGINIA AVE.

TENTH

BUREAU OF INTERNAL REVENUE

NEW NATIONAL MUSEUM

ELEVENTH

POST OFFICE

TWELFTH

MADISON DRIVE

THIRTEENTH

DEPARTMENT OF AGRICULTURE

C

DEPARTMENT OF COMMERCE

FOURTEENTH

BUREAU OF ENGRAVING AND PRINTING

THE Ellipse

ELLIPSE ROAD

CONSTITUTION AVE.

WASHINGTON MONUMENT

FIFTEENTH

INDEPENDENCE AVE.

ORIENTAL FLOWERING CHERRY TREES

Tidal Basin

palacios

62

but also an important publishing center. In its reports and papers you will find in accurate form, sometimes popularly and sometimes technically expressed, almost the whole progress of human knowledge. Exchange of these for publications of other scientific organizations, here and abroad, has brought such a heavy flow of learned papers and books that special arrangements had to be made to deposit them with the Library of Congress.

The Smithsonian has, all told, the incredible total of 44 million catalogued objects, 647,000 of which were added in 1957 alone. For many years, scientific and historical exhibit material piled in so fast, and became so crowded in the limited exhibit space, that the Smithsonian was nicknamed "Uncle Sam's Attic."

The Smithsonian has more "firsts" and "originals" than any other museum in America, including patent models of many inventions that Russia claims! Here, too, are full-size earliest locomotives, automobiles, bicycles, and carriages, the most complete collection of U.S. stamps and coins, huge skeletons of prehistoric reptiles, more gems—including the Hope diamond which was donated by Harry Winston last year—and minerals than have ever been assembled in one place, and the largest display of meteorites, those mysterious visitors from outer space.

Because the Smithsonian pioneered in aerodynamics, it is only natural that its collection of planes and other items related to man's conquest of the air is unexcelled anywhere. Lion of them all, of course, is the Wright brothers' original plane, *Kitty Hawk*, in which man made his first controlled and sustained flight. Almost equally the focus of attention is the *Spirit of St. Louis*, the small craft which carried Lindbergh on the first solo flight across the Atlantic. These can be contrasted with the U. S. Air Force's rocket-propelled plane, the Bell X-1, first craft to penetrate the sonic barrier.

Washington's National Zoological Park had its origin in a few pens and corrals that once stood near the Smithsonian's administration building. Some of the animals, reptiles, and birds were gifts to the Presidents, who turned them over to the Smithsonian so that they might be used as models by taxidermists and scientists preparing exhibits. But odors and insects made the creatures' presence intolerable, so a new site was secured in Rock Creek Park. This has since grown until Washington's Zoo, still a division of the Smithsonian, is now second in size and completeness to the Bronx Zoo in New York. In its Bird House is a talking myna bird which, they say, can spot a Congressman on sight, and follow through with that most pregnant of Washington queries: "What about the appropriation?"

Since 1946 the Smithsonian's responsibilities have been extended to the tropics. In that year it was given charge of the Canal Zone Biological Area, a tropical jungle preserve, teeming with bird and insect life, on an island in a lake in the Canal Zone.

The Smithsonian is internationally renowned for its museums, art galleries, and its extensive research, explorations, and publications.

Above figures in the Smithsonian's First Ladies Hall are, left to right, Mrs. James Monroe, Mrs. Maria Monroe Gouverneur, Mrs. John Quincy Adams.

Every First Lady since the administration of William Howard Taft
has given a dress to the Smithsonian's First Ladies
Hall. Soon after the presentation of Mrs. Taft's inaugural
dress in 1912, other dresses were received from former
First Ladies or their descendants. Each exhibit case contains dresses representing a span of 25 years, set against
a background that is typical of the furnishings and fixtures of
the period. Today the collection represents changes
in American costume from the time of George Washington to the
present day. Figures in the photograph above,
left to right, are those of Mrs. Harding and Mrs. Coolidge.

Period from 1869 to 1893 is represented above. Figure of Julia Grant is at far right. Central figure below is that of Angelica Van Buren.

Era of hoop skirt and figure of Mary Todd Lincoln, far right, is pictured above. Edith Bolling Wilson, below left, is in the 1893–1921 exhibit.

President and Mrs. Eisenhower inspect Mrs. Eisenhower's wedding gown, which she donated to the Smithsonian. Below left is her inaugural gown.

James Smithson, an Englishman who had never been in the United States, died in 1829, bequeathing his fortune of $550,000 to this country "to found at Washington, under the name of the Smithsonian Institution, an establishment for the increase and diffusion of knowledge among men." After his death Smithson's body was brought to America and now rests in a little chapel, above, within the redstone castle-like administration building, completed in 1852. He is thus the only important personage buried in downtown Washington.

Some of the earliest power machines are on display in the Smithsonian, above. The steam turbine is on exhibit below.

One of the most famous exhibits is Charles Lindbergh's *The Spirit of St. Louis*. Oldest complete locomotive used in America is "John Bull," below.

Exhibits are carefully prepared and maintained by Smithsonian's expert staff. Hopi Indian snake dance exhibit is a popular one.

Aerial view shows the Natural History Building (U. S. National Museum) in the foreground, which contains, among others, outstanding collections and exhibits in biology, geology, and anthropology as well as the National Collection of Fine Arts including work by Albert P. Ryder, Childe Hassam, John LaFarge, James McNeill Whistler, and others. The Museum also houses one of the largest natural history libraries in the country. The beautiful National Gallery of Art, shown beyond it in the photograph above, contains priceless works of art that include paintings, sculpture, prints, drawings. The magnificent Mellon, Kress, Widener, Dale, Rosenwald collections donated to the Gallery have helped to make it one of the leading museums of painting and sculpture in the world. Pictures on the opposite page provide closer views of these Smithsonian buildings: Natural History Building, top, National Gallery of Art, bottom.

The Alba Madonna by Raphael, which cost more than a million dollars, was purchased by Andrew Mellon and donated to the National Gallery.

This room also contains paintings from the Mellon collection. Works of Sir Joshua Reynolds and George Romney are represented here.

Pictures above are a part of the famed Mellon collection. Painting at left in the room is Rembrandt's Young Man at a Table.

The Freer Gallery of Art has a notable collection of Oriental paintings, sculptures, stones, bronzes and pottery, as well as the work of American artists including James McNeill Whistler. The bizarre Peacock Room, designed by Whistler for a London shipbuilder has, among other things, golden peacocks with crystal eyes and is a favorite with visitors. Other Americans represented in this collection are Homer, Sargent, Dewing, and Thayer.

WHAT VISITORS TO WASHINGTON WILL SEE

If the visitor to the national capital arrives by train, he cannot but be awed with the Union Station's main waiting room, designed after ancient Rome's imposing Baths of Caracalla, or vastly impressed by the main concourse, planned to handle Inauguration Day throngs of 100,000 to 120,000 people. However, during World War II, this number poured through the big terminal daily. Each twenty-four hours some 200 trains arrive and depart on seven different railroads, bearing Pullman cars to and from such distant places as Canada, Chicago, and Florida.

Washington's National Airport, one of the nation's busiest, is only 3½ miles from the heart of the capital, and therefore is the closest-in of any major city landing field. It is also the only civil airport owned by the federal government. Landing fees and concessions since 1941 have virtually equalled the cost of its construction, some $16,000,000. But it is overcrowded, and a larger field, farther out, is now being built.

In addition to the headquarters of a multitude of government agencies, Washington offers a vast array of interesting places to visit and things to see outside the government. Opposite Lafayette Square, social center of the capital during the gaslight era, is ancient St. John's Church, where many Presidents have worshipped since 1816. It is now somewhat over-

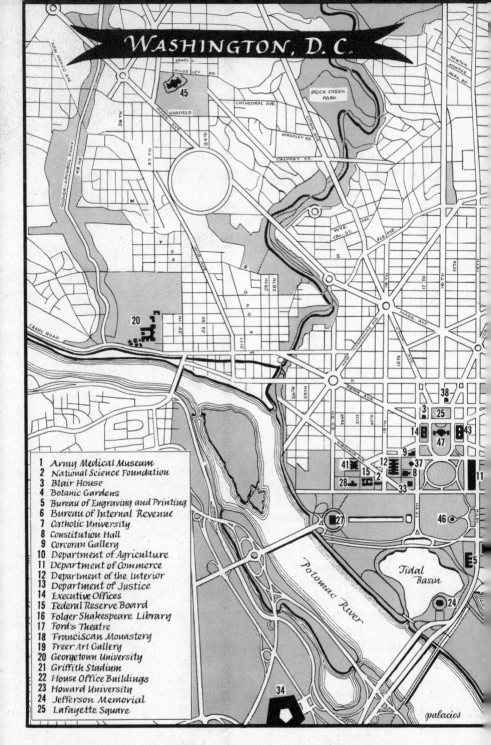

WASHINGTON, D.C.

1 Army Medical Museum
2 National Science Foundation
3 Blair House
4 Botanic Gardens
5 Bureau of Engraving and Printing
6 Bureau of Internal Revenue
7 Catholic University
8 Constitution Hall
9 Corcoran Gallery
10 Department of Agriculture
11 Department of Commerce
12 Department of the Interior
13 Department of Justice
14 Executive Offices
15 Federal Reserve Board
16 Folger Shakespeare Library
17 Ford's Theatre
18 Franciscan Monastery
19 Freer Art Gallery
20 Georgetown University
21 Griffith Stadium
22 House Office Buildings
23 Howard University
24 Jefferson Memorial
25 Lafayette Square

palacios

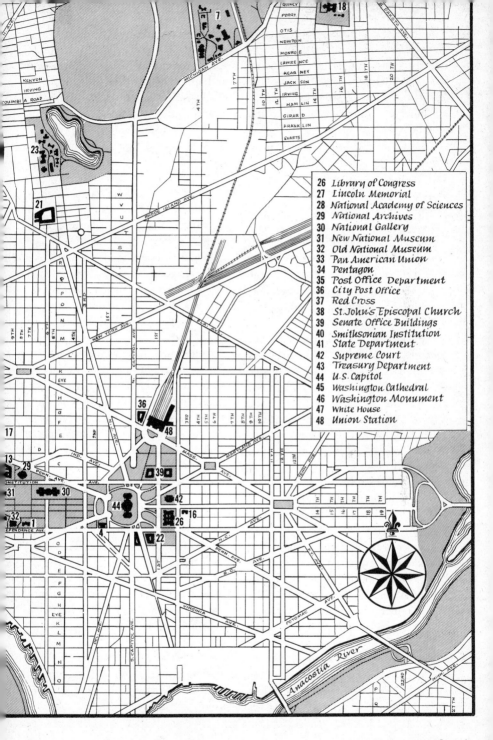

26 Library of Congress
27 Lincoln Memorial
28 National Academy of Sciences
29 National Archives
30 National Gallery
31 New National Museum
32 Old National Museum
33 Pan American Union
34 Pentagon
35 Post Office Department
36 City Post Office
37 Red Cross
38 St. John's Episcopal Church
39 Senate Office Buildings
40 Smithsonian Institution
41 State Department
42 Supreme Court
43 Treasury Department
44 U.S. Capitol
45 Washington Cathedral
46 Washington Monument
47 White House
48 Union Station

shadowed by the next-door, marble office-palace of the AFL-CIO, symbol that Washington has also become the union labor capital. By way of contrast, the headquarters of the U. S. Chamber of Commerce stands within a stone's throw.

The Dolly Madison House, once used by the Cosmos Club, is now the National Aeronautics and Space Administration. Facing it across Lafayette Square, the Decatur House, built by the hero of Tripoli shortly before he was killed in a duel, has retained its early nineteenth-century charm. It recently was deeded to the Navy for formal entertaining. The carriage shed behind it contains a real gem of a Navy museum.

Sixteenth is one of Washington's most dashing avenues: it is broad and well landscaped and is the motorists' dream, having neither break nor curve from the White House to the District line, and along it you will pass many important places that are almost constantly in the news. The Russian Embassy, for instance, is across the street from the headquarters of the National Geographic Society, whose "Explorer's Hall" is open free to visitors. A little farther up the street are the National Education Association, American Nature Association, Sons of the American Revolution, American Association for the Advancement of Science, and the Carnegie Institution.

Some of the elegant old mansions of Washington's former "Gold Coast" (Massachusetts Avenue between Du Pont and Sheridan Circles) have been taken over by embassies and clubs. In this area Evalyn Walsh ("Father Struck It Rich") McLean, Larz Anderson, Richard Townsend, and other millionaires entertained in the grand manner during the early years of the twentieth century. Anderson House, headquarters of the Society of the Cincinnati, makes its mirrored ballroom available to the State Department for diplomatic receptions. The lavish Townsend mansion houses the Cosmos Club, a social organization of noted scientists, economists, writers, and others.

When residents and visitors alike want a good seafood dinner they head for "The Wharf," as Washington's short but picturesque waterfront is known. "The Wharf" actually means a section of Maine Avenue, not far from the cherry trees around the Tidal Basin. Its score or more eating places range from large seafood restaurants with elaborate menus to small oyster bars where patrons sit on stools before oilcloth counters, eating oysters or clams on the half-shell.

Another absolute "must" for visitors to Washington is the National Archives, in the Federal Triangle, wherein are enshrined the three foundation stones of the Republic—the original Declaration of Independence, the Constitution, and the Bill of Rights. These priceless documents, sealed in bronze and glass cases filled with helium, are screened from harmful rays by special filters. In case of enemy attack, they can be lowered, within minutes, into a large underground safe that is bombproof, fireproof, and shockproof.

A glimpse of the Washington Monument is seen here from behind the Pan American Union, one of Washington's most beautiful buildings.

Symbolic sculptures adorn front of the Pan American Union building,
dedicated to friendship among the 21 American republics.

Fountain in the inner court was designed
by Gertrude Vanderbilt Whitney.

Pan American Union has been scene
of many historic and social events.

85

Three beautiful stained glass windows designed by Louis Tiffany decorate
the auditorium of the American Red Cross Building.

Corcoran Art Gallery, above, has a magnificent collection of American art.
Memorial Continental Hall, right, is the headquarters of the D.A.R.

The Bureau of Engraving and Printing, above and right, prints our currency, postage stamps, government bonds, liquor and tobacco stamps, licenses, and revenue stamps. Tours through the building, which houses some six thousand workers, show visitors many of the delicate and exact processes involved in the printing of our paper currency from the raw paper and making of ink to the finished notes.

Federal Reserve Building is headquarters for Federal Reserve System.

Department of Commerce Building
includes Patent Office, above.

Historic Treasury drafts are exhibited in the United States Treasury Building, above, including the one for $7,200,000 to Russia for Alaska.

This spectacular night view of the Capitol is from the Washington Monument. The Mall and the Smithsonian buildings can be seen here.

National Academy of Sciences and National Research Council have their headquarters in this handsome building.

Tour through the F.B.I. offices in the Department of Justice Buildings, above, is popular with visitors.

Offices of the Secretary of State are in the new State Department Building. Exhibits of important treaties, state papers, are in Document Room.

The National Archives Building preserves thousands
of our precious historical documents from the time of the Revolution.

President Truman, right, was present at the instal-
lation of the Declaration of Independence in National Archives Building.

Declaration of Independence, Constitution,
and Bill of Rights are carefully sealed in bronze cases.

Impish Puck
decorates garden of the Folger.

Owned and administered by Amherst College, the Folger Shakespeare
Library was endowed by Henry Clay Folger and contains
250,000 volumes about the 16th and 17th century, including
some of the rarest editions of Shakespeare's work. The Elizabethan interior of the building is a delightful surprise to visitors.

97

Labor Unions

Organized labor in the United States now has a membership totalling some 17,000,000 workers. Headquarters for the American Federation of Labor and Congress of Industrial Organizations, more familiarly known as AFL-CIO, is the handsome building on the right, on Sixteenth Street. Bottom right, is the conference room on the 8th floor and photographs on the opposite page show the lobby, top, and the office of President George Meany.

99

Headquarters for the International Brotherhood of Teamsters is the building above. Notice reflection of Capitol on entrance, below.

Above is headquarters for the International Union of Operating Engineers.
Colorful John L. Lewis is shown below at a Congressional hearing.

Blair House, at the left, frequently referred to as the nation's guest house, has considerable historic interest attached to it. It was here that Colonel Robert E. Lee was asked by Abraham Lincoln, through Mr. Blair, to accept command of the Union Armies. Lee of course refused and later wrote: ". . . though opposed to secession and deprecating war, I could take no part in an invasion of the Southern States." Constitution Hall, at the top, was built by the Daughters of the American Revolution and has a seating capacity of 4,000.

Dr. James T. Gallahorn, Jr., right, Administrative Principal, welcomes new students to the Americanization School, which assists both native and foreign born students to adjust to an ever-changing American life.

United States Marine Corps War Memorial recalls the flag raising
at Iwo Jima and honors marines who have given their lives since 1775.

First Division Memorial honors Division men who died in World War I.

This striking Navy-Marine Memorial is in West Potomac Park.

Taft Memorial, 100 feet high, has a carillon of 27 bells at top.

Titanic Memorial honors gallant men who went down with the ship.

Simón Bolívar, Venezuela's champion
of liberty, is honored above.

Second Division dead of World
War I are remembered here.

This Union Square monument honors
Civil War's General George Meade.

Equestrian statue of Washington
stands in Washington Circle.

The American Legion's thousands march up Pennsylvania and Constitution Avenues along the famous "route of heroes." Note the colors of the Armed Forces, nearing turn at Fifteenth and Pennsylvania Avenue.

Trans—portation

If a visitor arrives by train in Washington, he emerges at handsome Union Station, left, and gets his first glimpse of the Capitol facing it. The visitor arriving by plane lands at Washington National Airport, one of the busiest in the world, and just three and a half miles from downtown Washington. Two forms of transportation which the visitor no longer sees are the trolley cars along Pennsylvania Avenue and the monorail which shuttled back and forth between the Senate Office Building and the Capitol. A new subway now ferries Senators to and from the New and Old Senate Office buildings and the Capitol.

The handsome building above is the Carnegie Institution in Washington.

This new building which houses the District Court is frequently the scene
of the ceremony at which new citizens take the oath of allegiance.

Miss Frances G. Knight, Director of the Passport Office, is shown here in her office. Below are the extensive Passport Office files.

Department of the Interior has excellent exhibits relating to national parks, native arts and crafts.

The Department of Health, Education, and Welfare, formerly the Federal Security Agency, is above. Below is the block-long, new General Accounting Office.

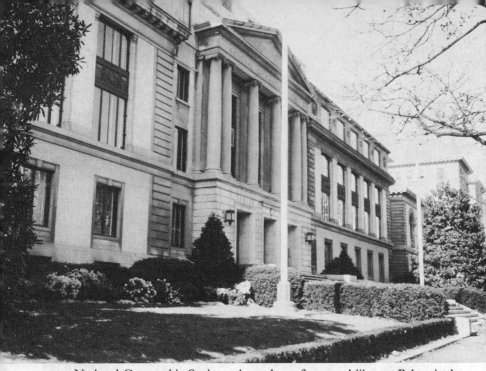

National Geographic Society, above, has a fine travel library. Below is the Museum of the Society of the Cincinnati. Its first president was Washington.

Established by Act of Congress in 1901, the National Bureau of Standards is constantly engaged in research and development projects of practical value to national defense and the American consumer. Technician in the photograph at the top is mounting specimens of thread that will be tested for the Army's office of the Quartermaster General. Ralph Stair, physicist and principal designer, is shown inspecting the spectroradiometer, which measures solar radiation. Glass molder, right, is heating glass so that impurities can be removed by snipping them out with shears.

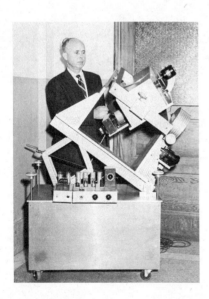

Perhaps the largest and most impressive group of public buildings anywhere is that to be found in the Federal Triangle area on the north side
of the Mall. The Department of Commerce Building, the old and the new
Post Office Department buildings, Department of Justice, Bureau
of Internal Revenue, Federal Trade Commission, Department of Labor,
and the beautiful National Archives are all found here.

One of the most exciting tours that a visitor can take in Washington is the one through the headquarters of the Federal Bureau of Investigation in the Department of Justice Building. Conducted tours include an explanation of the fingerprint system, stories of how notorious criminals have been caught, a visit to the scientific crime laboratory, and finally a demonstration of marksmanship on the range in the building. FBI men are thoroughly trained in modern crime detection methods.

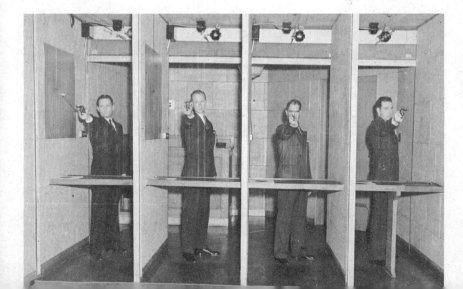

The late President Roosevelt is shown here traditionally starting
Washington's baseball season by throwing out the first ball.

Washington's summertime Watergate concerts are very popular.

The White House and Washington Monument are sharply revealed
by the brilliant Fourth of July fireworks.

Headquarters for the American Pharmaceutical Association is the building above, which has many fascinating exhibits.

Lincoln Memorial's Reflecting Pool provides fine skating when the winter temperature drops.

This charming six-room home on Irving Street, N.E., is the only completely round house in Washington.

The Scottish Rite Temple, a magnificent building designed after the Greek tradition, contains an extensive Masonic library.

George Washington Masonic National Memorial, in Alexandria, Virginia,
honors the most famous of all American Masons.

CHURCHES, COLLEGES, AND EMBASSIES

Upper Massachusetts Avenue contains three of the Capital's most unusual and important places of worship. Like something out of *The Arabian Nights*, the slender minaret of the Mosque and Islamic Center soars far above the treetops of Rock Creek Park. Built by the fifteen Moslem countries with diplomatic missions in Washington, the Mosque each Friday noon summons the Moslem faithful in the city to prayer.

A little farther up Massachusetts Avenue, in a residential section, rises the smooth white dome and classic profile of St. Sophia Greek Orthodox Cathedral, a newcomer to the Washington scene.

But no place of worship in the Capital possesses such a commanding location as the Cathedral of St. Peter and St. Paul (Episcopal), familiarly known as the Washington Cathedral, whose Gothic spires and splendid flying buttresses emerge from a wooded close on the summit of Mt. St. Alban. In chapels within its enormous crypt are buried President Woodrow Wilson, Admiral Dewey, and other famous persons.

You may be surprised to find that in some of these chapels services are being conducted in Russian Orthodox, Jewish, Polish National Catholic, Ukrainian Orthodox, and other creeds. Because it was chartered as a "house of prayer for all people," the Cathedral has mothered many congregations until they could find homes of their own. The Cathedral is unique also in that it is the seat of two bishops: the Presiding Bishop of the Protestant Episcopal Church of the United States, and the Bishop of the Diocese of Washington.

Over in the northeast part of the District are two noteworthy Roman Catholic institutions. The National Shrine of the Immaculate Conception, adjoining the grounds of Catholic University, will be the largest Roman Catholic church in the Western Hemisphere, and the seventh largest church in the world. The nearby Franciscan Monastery, dedicated to the preservation of shrines in the Holy Lands, has not only one of the most colorful gardens in the Capital, but also amazing reproductions of a section of the Catacombs, the Grotto of Bethlehem, the Gethsemane Valley, and the Tomb of the Blessed Virgin, giving the visitor a very accurate idea of these places.

Of the Capital's many famous churches, one other, St. Paul's Episcopal, deserves special mention because its graveyard, Rock Creek Cemetery, contains perhaps the finest statue in Washington. This masterpiece of Augustus Saint-Gaudens, erected by historian Henry Adams in memory of his wife, bears no inscription, but is generally known as "Grief" or "The Peace of God."

On a hillside overlooking the Potomac, the spires and towers of Georgetown University, oldest of Roman Catholic institutions of higher learning in the United States, somewhat resemble those of Heidelberg along the Rhine. When John Carroll founded the college in 1789, before Washington became the national capitol, he seriously considered Capitol Hill as a possible site, but decided it was "too far in the country."

Georgetown's 100-acre campus includes an astronomical observatory and a seismograph, the latter an important listening post for earthquakes. Its School of Foreign Service has launched many diplomats on their careers. Georgetown has made headlines as one of the important universities to drop inter-collegiate football.

George Washington University, dating from 1821, would please Washington who expressed a wish that the Nation's Capital have a school "to which the youth and talents from all parts thereof might be sent for the completion of their education in all branches of polite literature; in arts and sciences, in acquiring knowledge in the principles of politics and good government."

In Howard University, the Capital has a leading institution of higher education operated primarily for Negroes; however, it has a student body comprising all major races (including white) and creeds, from almost every state in the Union and thirty foreign countries.

American University, Catholic University, Gallaudet College (for the deaf), Trinity College, and, at nearby College Park, Maryland, the University of Maryland, are other important schools of higher learning in the area.

When Washingtonians speak of "Embassy Row" they refer to a cluster of embassies and legations—Italy, Mexico, Spain, Poland, Cuba, Lithuania, Netherlands, Hungary, and Jordan—along or near Sixteenth Street on Meridian Hill. However, since the British built a veritable red-brick palace near Observatory Circle, central and upper Massachusetts Avenue has been the fashionable address for foreign missions. About two-thirds of the eighty-five nations having diplomatic representatives in Washington are grouped along this beautiful boulevard, shaded by more lindens than is Berlin's celebrated "Unter den Linden".

This magnificent gothic structure is the Cathedral of St. Peter and St. Paul, Protestant Episcopal, popularly called the Washington Cathedral.

The sixth largest church in the world, the Washington Cathedral is 525 feet long, 275 feet wide, has a ceiling reaching 102 feet.

St. John's Episcopal Church, called "the Church of the Presidents" because many have worshiped here, reserves a pew for the President and his family.

The Church of the Latter-Day Saints (Mormon) on Sixteenth Street is
made of marble that came from Utah.

Mosque on Embassy Row

From the graceful minaret of
this Mosque, which faces Mecca, may
be heard the chant, broadcast by
loud speaker, summoning the faithful
to prayer. Built by fifteen
Eastern nations, the Mosque has
an adjoining wing called the
Islamic Institute that welcomes
students—whatever their faith—
to the classrooms,
library, and museum.

The Franciscan Monastery Memorial Church of the Holy Land has many reproductions of the sacred shrines of the Holy Land.

In the Franciscan Monastery's Rosary garden there are two statues: one of St. Francis, the other of St. Christopher, above.

Georgetown University, oldest Catholic university in the country, was founded by John Carroll in 1789.

The Catholic University of America occupies over eighty acres on one of the highest points in the District of Columbia.

McMahon Hall of Catholic University houses various laboratories, classrooms, administrative offices, and an auditorium.

Howard University has an attractive campus, about 4,000 students.

George Washington University has a student enrollment of some 9,000.

The Brazilian Embassy, on Whitehaven Street, N.W., contains a magnificent marble stairway in the entrance hall.

Russian Embassy was owned by the wife of the designer of famed Pullman car. Spanish Embassy, right, is at 2700 Sixteenth Street, N.W.

This large, handsome mansion is the Turkish Embassy, which stands on the southwest corner of Twenty-third Street.

The tour of embassies and legations is very popular with visitors to Washington. Above is the Luxemburg Embassy.

This attractive building is the Venezuelan Embassy, located along Embassy Row at 2445 Massachusetts Avenue.

MILITARY WASHINGTON

Except in time of war, when military uniforms are seen everywhere on the streets of the Capital, the military aspect of Washington is usually well overshadowed by civil functions and activity. Yet from here top decisions control our far-flung Army, Navy, and Air Force. In Washington, too, you will find such quasi-military bodies as the Selective Service System, which brings men into the armed services, and the Veterans Administration, which takes care of them, if needed, after they leave.

The Army Medical Center at Walter Reed Hospital, the Naval Medical Center in Bethesda, Maryland, and the Armed Forces Institute of Pathology are outstanding agencies devoted to the physical welfare of both active and retired military personnel.

In Arlington National Cemetery, once the plantation of the Lee family, the Virginia side of the Potomac possesses the nation's most famous burial ground. Its Tomb of the Unknowns, formerly called the Tomb of the Unknown Soldier, honors servicemen of World War I, World War II and the Korean War, and is guarded day and night by an armed sentry. It is perhaps America's most revered shrine.

The Washington area also plays an active part in the nation's defense through its own air bases, military posts, and barracks, as well as a navy yard. The latter, now known as the U. S. Naval Gun Factory, is the capital's only sizeable heavy industry, as well as the world's largest naval ordnance plant. An undeclared war with Tripoli and the threat of a war with France brought the yard into existence on October 2, 1799, when the streets of Washington were mere wagon trails and the young U. S. Navy was a handful of wooden ships. With the passing of battleships and other big-gun craft, more and more of the yard's activities turn toward development of rockets, guided missiles, and other modern weapons.

Not far away, at the Marine Barracks, you may witness on sunny Friday afternoons the "Sunset Tatoo," to the stirring music of the "Stars and Stripes Forever," and the "Washington Post March." These and other great military airs were written by former bandmaster of the Barracks, John Philip Sousa.

Fort Leslie J. McNair, one of the Army's oldest posts and the present site of the National War College, and Fort Myers, headquarters of the military district of Washington, are "forts" in name only, but each performs important military training functions, as well as offering pleasant quarters for some of the high Army "brass" stationed in the area. The Bolling Field Air Force Base and the Anacostia Naval Air Station, both somewhat outdated, are the District's only military landing fields. Andrews Air Base, in nearby Maryland, really protects the capital from enemy air attack.

Massachusetts Avenue makes a wide swing around a circular park containing the residence of the Chief of Naval Operations and the U. S. Naval Observatory. The latter has the important task of computing accurate time for the United States and for all the ships at sea. Star observations, made daily, provide the data for computations down to one-hundredth of a second. This may seem to be slicing time pretty thin, but such precision is needed for electronic devices now used by the military services, and for special scientific purposes elsewhere.

On a high point, just west of Georgia Avenue, stands historic Fort Stevens, one of the ring of forts that encircled Washington during the Civil War. President Lincoln stood exposed on its parapets during the repulse of General Early's Confederate raid, the only time a President of the United States has been under enemy military fire while in office. A junior Union officer shocked his superiors by ordering the commander-in-chief to get down, but Lincoln promptly obeyed!

Biggest and most renowned of military establishments in Washington is the Pentagon, headquarters of the Department of Defense. Washington law limits building heights to twelve stories or less, so the capital has no office skyscrapers, but it still possesses, in the sprawling Pentagon, the world's largest office building.

Aviators can spot its immense, five-sided mass at any altitude. Radar easily picks it up in foul weather. Nevertheless, nobody knows *exactly where it is!* That is, nobody knows officially. While the building rests firmly on the Virginia side of the Potomac, the Pentagon's mailing address is Washington 25, D.C. Office telephones are linked to the city's largest phone exchange (LIberty 5–6700), but pay phones in the corridors bear Arlington, Va. numbers. Arlington courts settle traffic violations on its roadways and parking lots, but police of the General Services Administration, with headquarters in Washington, keep order in its labyrinthian hallways. Washingtonians are used to this sort of thing, but it bewilders outsiders.

The tombs of President Woodrow Wilson, Admiral George Dewey, and prominent churchmen are to be found in Washington Cathedral.

The Pentagon

This five-story, five-sided building is the headquarters of the Defense Department. Largest office building in the world, the Pentagon covers 29 acres, contains 17½ miles of corridors, houses 30,000 workers, and has a parking lot that accommodates 8,000 cars! The building is open to the public and well worth a visit.

Striking group of buildings, above, is Naval Medical Center in nearby Bethesda. Army Medical Center includes nationally known Walter Reed Hospital, below.

Tomb of the Unknowns in Arlington is a simple, beautiful memorial to American servicemen who died in World Wars I and II and the Korean War.

Impressive Arlington Memorial Amphitheatre, right, in which
Memorial Day services are held, was fashioned
after the Theatre of Dionysus in Athens. The east
façade with its Corinthian
colonnade overlooks Washington and the Potomac.

Mast of the battleship Maine, sunk in
Havana harbor, is in Arlington.

The unknown dead of the Civil War
are remembered in this memorial.

Among the famous Americans buried in Arlington National Cemetery
are General Pershing, William Jennings Bryan, Admiral Peary.

The Lee Mansion in Arlington with its magnificent Doric columns commands a fine view of Washington. Below is the family dining room.

The charming room above is the drawing room. Restoration of the Mansion has been carefully done and is still going on.

The generous fireplace in the winter kitchen under the north wing helped to warm the rooms above during the cold months.

Terrestrial globe in the schoolroom is one of the most interesting original objects in the Mansion. Bedroom above is handsomely furnished.

WASHINGTON'S PARKS AND ENVIRONS

No city in America, and few in the world, can come near matching Washington's marvelous system of parks and gardens, large and small. Much credit goes to that imaginative genius, Major Pierre Charles L'Enfant, whom George Washington chose to work out the street and landscape scheme of the new capital. L'Enfant was perhaps the first to realize that here might be a great city and not just a haven for beleaguered office holders. So he made no little plans, and history has fulfilled his dreams.

Visiting motorists may curse L'Enfant as they attempt to thread their way through traffic, but the circles, diagonal avenues, malls, and parkways that confuse the stranger allow easy access, for residents, to any part of the city.

Pride and joy of all District residents is Rock Creek Park. A bit of wilderness close to home, it is a rugged and densely forested ravine that defied development, and thus much of it remains as it was in pioneer days. This natural outdoor playground, in some places more than a mile wide, now extends from the Potomac River well into Maryland.

Near the mouth of Rock Creek, Robert Fulton tested an early model of his steamship. Here today you will see the ancient, moss-covered locks of the Chesapeake & Ohio Canal, a waterway that was to run from Georgetown to the West and rival the Erie Canal. Begun in 1828, it reached Cumberland, Maryland, but finally succumbed to floods and railroad competition.

The banks of the winding Anacostia River have been set aside as a park, although frequent floods prevents full development of this valley's natural charm. On high land along the west bank spreads the National

Arboretum, an unsullied woodland dedicated to the study of every type of tree, shrub, and bush, native or exotic, that will grow in the Washington climate. Its masses of brilliant flowering azaleas, some gifts from Holland, rival the better known Tidal Basin cherry blossoms as a spring flower show. Across the river, ponds of the Kenilworth Aquatic Gardens burst into acres of loveliness in June, when thousands of water lilies and lotus are in full bloom.

Not far from Washington are scores of places that rival in interest some of the wonders of the capital. At Great Falls, a few miles up the Potomac, the river plunges through one of the most spectacular gorges in the East. Bethesda, Maryland, is fast becoming the nation's most important medical center. Here the huge National Institutes of Health adjoin the spreading Naval Medical Center, while nearby are numerous clinics and small manufacturers of medical equipment.

Downriver, the charming old city of Alexandria, "home town" of George Washington and Robert E. Lee, is still a seaport. The tall shaft of the George Washington Masonic National Memorial is a landmark. It rises from Shooter's Hill, once considered as a site for the Capitol. At Gadsby's Tavern Washington once attended banquets and balls, and around the corner, Carlyle House is much the same as it was when British General Braddock here planned his ill-fated campaign against the French at Fort Duquesne.

Enroute to Mount Vernon, along a splendid parkway that runs close to the Potomac, you will see on the Maryland side the weathered ramparts of a fortress rising from the water's edge. This is Fort Washington, an imposing bastion, but it never saw any enemy action.

Walk through the gates of Mount Vernon, home of the first President, and the centuries seem to fall away. You are back again in the days when the southern plantation was more than a place to live, when it was to its owner and guests a gracious way of life. Surrounding the mansion you will see all the things—stables, barn, greenhouses, cobbler shop, dairy, smokehouse, laundry, spinning house, repair sheds, slave quarters, gardens, and office—that made each plantation an almost self-supporting community.

Many of the furnishings in the mansion are original, others have been reproduced through painstaking research. A sketch on a long-lost insurance policy, for instance, enabled the staff to restore the large greenhouse. Eighteenth century bricks removed from the White House, when it was strengthened with concrete and steel during the Truman administration, were used in the greenhouse reconstruction.

Farther down the winding Potomac, but still within the Washington sight-seeing area, is Gunston Hall, the beautiful estate of George Mason, author of the Virginia Bill of Rights and Constitution. Gunston Hall is worth visiting, not only for its historic associations but also to see what are probably the largest and finest boxwood hedges in America.

Rock Creek Park, a woodland retreat of some 1800 acres, stretches through the heart of the city and offers many recreational facilities.

National Zoological Park, under the direction of the Smithsonian, contains one
of the most unusual collections of rare animals and birds in the world.

Popular with Washingtonians is the President's Cup Regatta held off Hains Point on the Potomac River. Above is the Sail Boat Division.

Fifteen miles northwest of Washington the Potomac River forms the Great Falls, cascading over granite rocks and passing through a gorge.

Washington wrote his correspondence and managed his affairs from the library of Mount Vernon.

Nelly Custis' childhood high chair can be seen in the family dining room.

Georgian in style, Mount Vernon, the home of George Washington, is one of our most lovely historic houses.

The music room, made especially for Nelly Custis, contains the harpsichord Washington imported from London for her.

The west parlor contains a number of interesting pieces—
among them an English card table and an Adam mirror.

The clock on the stair landing is part
of the original furnishings.

The banquet hall in Mount Vernon is
a story and a half high.

These homes overlook Georgetown's once thriving Chesapeake & Ohio Canal. Below is the Georgetown skyline.

The new Atomic Energy Commission
Building near Germantown, Maryland, is
not open to the public and is one of
the most carefully guarded buildings
in the country. Armed guards
and intricate alarm systems protect
the vital work being done. All papers
to be burned are consigned to the
incinerator under armed guard.

Photo Credits

Photograph credits read from left to right and top to bottom
Picture Position: T—Top; M—Middle; B—Bottom; L—Left; C—Center; R—Right.

© by JAMES R. DUNLOP, Inc. 8, 9(T), 12, 13, 20, 27, 28(B-L), 29, 38, 39(T), 41–43, 48(T), 49, 51(B), 52–53, 55(T-R), 57(M-B), 58–59, 64–68, 69(B), 70–71, 84, 87, 92–94, 96–97, 102, 103(T), 104, 105(T-R), 110, 121, 127, 131, 133(B-R), 134, 135(T-L), 143, 145(T-R, B), 153–159

GILOON AGENCY 44(T)

© by HARRIS & EWING 11(B), 14, 15, 18, 21(B), 24(T, B-L), 30, 34(C, B), 35, 37(B), 44(B), 45(T), 46, 55(B-R), 56(T-L, B-L), 69(T), 74, 95(B), 105(T-L), 107, 111(B), 112, 115, 117(M), 119(T), 120(B), 142(T), 160(B)

HARRIS & EWING 10, 24(B-R), 34(T), 45(B-L), 89, 95(T), 103(B), 108(T), 109(B), 111(T), 113(M, B), 117(T, B), 119(B), 142(B-L, B-R)

THE LIBRARY OF CONGRESS 21(T)

CHARLES L. SHERMAN 72, 85(T-R, B-R), 106(B-R), 114, 126(T), 128–129, 133(B-L), 135(T-R, B), 136

SMITHSONIAN INSTITUTION 73(B)

J. WARING STINCHCOMB 9(B), 11(T), 16, 17, 19, 22, 23, 28(B-R), 36(T, B), 37(T), 39(B), 40, 45(B-R), 47, 49(B), 50, 51(T), 54, 56(R), 57(T), 60, 73(T), 75–78, 83, 86, 88, 90–91, 101(B), 105(B-L, B-R), 106(T-L, T-R, B-L), 108(B-L), 113(T), 116, 118, 120(T, M), 122, 125, 126(B), 130, 132, 133(T), 139–141, 144, 146–150

WIDE WORLD PHOTOS 28(T), 160(T)

© by WURTS BROTHERS 98–100, 101(T), 108(B-R)

Photograph of the Jefferson Memorial on following pages by Hubert A. Lowman

Index